I Bet You Didn't Know

I Bet You Didn't Know

The Story Behind My Praise

Simply Truth

Library of Congress Control Number:		2019904221
ISBN:	Hardcover	978-1-7960-2687-0
	Softcover	978-1-7960-2686-3
	eBook	978-1-7960-2685-6

Print information available on the last page.

Rev. date: 04/10/2019

To order additional copies of this book, contact:
Xlibris
1-888-795-4274
www.Xlibris.com
Orders@Xlibris.com
792156

ACKNOWLEDGEMENTS

I WANT TO Thank my Lord and Savior Jesus Christ. Before I knew your name, you knew mine. You suffered and died so that I could live. You loved me when I didn't love myself. Thank you for the gift of trials for without them, I would not be the woman I am today. I love you Lord.

Thank you to my wonderful husband. Your love for me is expressed daily through your kindness, patience, and respect. I love you Mr. Wright

I thank my children for loving me through my worst and supporting me through my better. Thank you for my beautiful grandchildren.

A special Thank You to Pastor Torrey Montgomery. Your biblical based teaching and leadership inspired and encouraged me to look beyond the now and embrace the NEXT.

Thank you to all those who supported me by investing your time, finances, and prayers. God Bless you

INTRODUCTION

THIS BOOK IS in no way intended to discredit anyone's integrity or character. This book is a true story about a young girl who endures the tragedies, difficulties, and trials of life. She experiences emotional and physical abuse at the age of fourteen; is faced with becoming a teenage mom at the age of seventeen; and at age eighteen lives through the tragic death of her mother.

The story about a broken young girl, who psychologically becomes a victim of sexual abuse and bears the burden of guilt and shame.

The story about how the young girl grows into a woman filled with anger, bitterness, envy, and unforgiveness and is led into a life of self-destruction.

The story about a woman who has an encounter with God and finds her identity through the Love of Jesus Christ.

This is my story

CHAPTER 1

The Beginning

I T IS SIMPLY amazing how the mind works. At age fifty, I began having childhood memories. Memories that were suppressed are being manifested in my mind. The memories are not filed with joy and laughter, but heartache and pain. My mind is open, and I began to ponder on how difficult it was for me being born with physical and visual impairments. I would like to share a few of these memories that are more vivid than others.

Due to physical impairment to my legs, I had to wear braces to learn to walk. Over time, my legs grew stronger and I no longer needed the braces. Unfortunately, the visual impairment was irreversible. Because I would fall over, trip over, and walk into anything in my pathway, my sister, Alexa, would sit me in a chair with side arms to keep me safe.

In pre-k my class would take daily walks. My teacher noticed that I had a problem with my vision, so she would hold my hand and guide me along the country road as we walked. I remember how she would allow me to step in a few water puddles for the fun of it. I wasn't treated any different from my classmates, but I knew I was.

In middle school, I played basketball and ran track. I knew it would be a challenge, but I was determined to be like everyone else. I hardly played in any of the ball games because

I struggled to see the ball. That didn't matter to me. I was happy to be a part of the team. Running track was a dare for me because light hindered my visual impairment even more. I remember I was attempting to jump a hurdle and couldn't see that I was jumping it backwards. That hurdle hit my shin bone and I thought it was broken. I didn't quit trying though. On the relay team, I didn't know if I stayed in my lane or not, but I ran anyway.

In high school, I remember how I would walk into poles, and trip up and down stairs. I could hear people laughing at me and I would laugh along with them, but on the inside, I was very angry, envious, and insecure. I just wanted to be normal.

THERE ALL THE TIME
Feeling all alone in a distant place
Longing for a touch and warm embrace
Not knowing where to go and not knowing what to do
When I heard Jesus say my child I love you
I am there all the time reaching out for your hand in mine
My child if you would just believe
My promises you will receive
Because I am there all the time
Reaching out for you hand in mine
My child if you would just believe
My promises you will receive
Pain deep within oh pain go away
Nothing but storm clouds when will I see a brighter day
Trials on every hand, burdens so hard to bear
When I heard Jesus say cast upon me your every care

I am there all the time reaching out for your hand in mine
My child if you would just believe my
promises you will receive
Because I am there all the time reaching
out for your hand in mine
My child if you would just believe my
promises you will receive
You are never alone because I am right there all the time
Wiping your tears away helping you
make it through the day
My child if you would just believe my
promises you will receive.

CHAPTER 2

It Happened to Me

IT WAS THE summer of 1978. I was fourteen and became very close friends with a young man named Anthony. He was my very first boyfriend. In the winter of the same year, Anthony would turn eighteen. To me, he was very handsome. I was skinny, wore thick glasses, and felt ugly and odd. Why Anthony chose me, I didn't know, but I was glad to be his girlfriend. Having someone that seemed to really like me, made me feel happy.

Anthony was an athlete in football and track and owned a car. There were times when he asked me to attend events with him. If the event was during the night, I would go. Anything during the day, I would make an excuse not to go. I didn't want to embarrass him by falling, tripping, or walking into things. Anthony did not know the severity of my impairment and I was not going to tell him. I was fourteen and a virgin when Anthony and I met. He was far more advanced in reference to the world of entertainment; clubbing, drinking, drugs, sex. I lost my virginity to Anthony at age fourteen.

Anthony and I were at his house when his mother made a statement "You better not get pregnant." That was the first time anyone had mentioned getting pregnant to me. What did that mean exactly? No one in my family had talked about it. All I knew is that once I had my first menstrual, Anthony began using condoms.

At age fifteen, I began going to the clubs with Anthony and smoking marijuana. No one ever told me it was wrong, so I did it. I loved to dance so clubbing was fun. Being on the dance floor, made me feel pretty and free from my inner pain. One night while Anthony and I were at the club, I saw a side of him I had never seen before. I had danced so much that I began sweating and walked outside to get some fresh air. There was a male friend of ours standing outside so I walked over to talk to him. As we stood there talking, Anthony came outside the club and joined us. After talking for a short time, we all went back inside.

The time had come for the club to close. As Anthony and I walked to his car, he began questioning me about why I was outside talking to our friend. The questions he asked me seemed very silly. I must have given him answers he did not want to hear. Anthony slapped me so hard. My glasses flew off my face and landed some place on the ground. I could not believe what had just happened. What had I done wrong? What had I said wrong? I began to cry as Anthony was looking for my glasses. He found them and they were broken. I cried all the way home. Anthony gave me several reasons as to why he hit me. One of the reasons being, "You should not have been talking to another man." I convinced myself that he was right to excuse his wrong. I told my mom that I had broken my glasses and she never questioned me as to how.

I was fifteen and still in a relationship with Anthony. My anger and insecurities had now partnered with fear. This young man that appeared to be stable and strong, was not the person I thought he was. His jealousy began to surface but his actions were all my fault. If only I was pretty and didn't have these thick glasses, dark skin, and this gap between my teeth, he would love me more. I felt so ugly on the inside. I wanted Anthony to love me so I told myself that I was going to try and act older so he would love me better.

It was the summer of 1980 and I had turned sixteen. Anthony and I were still in a relationship. I was trying to act older than I was, and clueless as to what I was doing or expected to do. Anthony was always friendly with the ladies, but I wasn't allowed to be friendly with any man other than him. I had broken up with him several times in the past, but we always got back together. On this one occasion, Anthony had gotten a little too friendly with one of the ladies, so I broke up with him.

Anthony started dating someone else and I thought I was going to die. I begged him to take me back, but he refused. The pain of that breakup seemed to hurt more than the physical pain he inflicted on me. We were no longer a couple but would continue sharing intimate moments with one another.

It was July of 1980 when I met James. James was visiting from California for the fourth of July holiday. I asked James his age and he told me he was twenty-two. He then asked my age and I told him I was seventeen soon to be eighteen. James was very handsome. I felt very ugly still. I was happy, once again, to get the attention of this handsome young man. I lied to James about my age because I did not want him to think I was too young and not like me. My first time ever feeling semen, would be my first intimate encounter with James. It would also be the start of a new life inside me. A new life that no one had explained to me. Janes left and went back home to California

August passed when I noticed I did not have a menstrual cycle. I didn't think much about it because no one had told me to expect it every month. It wasn't until I began feeling nauseated at the sight of food that I knew something wasn't right. I was academically smart in school, but very naive to the concepts of LIFE. I began researching my symptoms and to my surprise, I was pregnant. I knew in my heart that it was James's baby. I wrote a letter inform him of the news. I told no one else and waited for James to write me back. After not hearing from James, I told Anthony that I was pregnant, but I did not tell him everything.

I was scared and felt very alone. I did not want this pregnancy so I began to search out what I could do to not be pregnant. I read an article on abortion and what it meant to have one. I found a doctor in the yellow pages and scheduled an appointment. How I would pay for it, I did not know.

I was drying off from a bath, when my mom walked into the bathroom. She looked at me and asked? "Are you pregnant?" I was too afraid to say anything. My mom, said "If you are, you are going to live with Anthony and his parents." Hearing those words, heightened my anger, fear, and pain to a whole new level! At the same time, I felt relieved because my mom knew I was pregnant. After a few days had past, my mom came to my bedroom and said she was going to call and schedule an appointment for me to have an abortion. She didn't know I had one scheduled already, so I told her about it.

It was on October 17, 1980 when I went to a doctor appointment to have an abortion. The ride there was very silent and unusual. It was all going to be over soon. I would not be pregnant. No one would ever know that I was pregnant at sixteen. When we arrived, we checked in and waited. Finally, my name was called. I was led into a room where I was told to get undressed and lay on the table. The doctor came in and began to examine me. The thought "It will all be over soon" calmed my fear.

Upon completing the exam, the Dr. rolls his chair back, pulls off his gloves, and says to my mom "We cannot do the procedure because she it too far along." WHAT? "Can't do the procedure!" Was ringing in my mind. The rest of the doctor's statement was made clear to me when my mom said "Well, you are going to have a baby." What was I going to do with a child? I'm a child myself! My mom was so sweet and did all she knew to do for my comfort.

I continued attending Scheel. At times, I could see people looking at me whispering, but I didn't stop. I had this one classmate that walked with me, talked with me, and loved me just the way I was. Lavonda was very kind, gentle, and caring. She encouraged and inspired me in more ways than she would know. However, I was so angry and hated myself for being so stupid. A junior in high school and pregnant.

CHAPTER 3

My Little Angel

O N JANUARY 14, 1981, I turned seventeen years old and six months pregnant. On March 31, 1981, around five o'clock in the morning, I was awakened by sharp pains in my lower abdomen. I woke my mom and told her I was hurting. My mom's response was "Ok." I remember day breaking outside and it seemed as if that morning was the longest ever. My mom must have called my sister, Alexa, because she came over and drove me to the hospital. My sister stayed there with me and I was assigned a room.

No one had ever explained to me about the issues of life, and its consequences. At age seventeen, and for twenty-six hours, I experienced the pains of labor. My sister was there with me, but I wanted to see my momma. I should have been afraid, but on that day, I felt no anger, fear, nor loneliness. I felt a sense of peace and comfort within me.

At approximately seven fifteen AM on April 1, 1981. I gave birth to the most beautiful baby girl I had ever seen. I was a mom but felt like a little girl holding a baby doll. I was glad to not be pregnant anymore but wondered where my mom was because I hadn't seen her since leaving the house the day before. When my mom finally came into my hospital room, and walked over to my bed, the look she had on her face erased any concern I had in my mind. She had tears in her eyes and was rubbing her hands together as if she were trying to comfort herself. I can only imagine the fear my mom must have felt in knowing that her seven-teen year old baby was giving birth to a baby. My mom handled the circumstance the best way she knew how. I didn't know it until later, but my mom Prayed for me and that prayer covered me and gave me that peace and comfort I felt on that day. I remained in the hospital for four days.

When I arrived home, from the hospital, my sweet mom had my room all set up and ready for baby and me. I didn't know what I needed, but my mom did. With help from her, my granny, and my sisters I cared for my baby girl as best I knew how. Faith was like a little doll to me, but a living doll. Becoming a mom at seven-teen was strange and so unexpected for me. It felt new and fun for a while, but as time passed, my mom had to remind me that my child was my responsibility.

As I started the fall semester of my senior year, I began to feel like I was trapped. I had feelings of anger, pain, frustration, low self-esteem, regret, envy, and self-pity. I needed the freedom to do what I wanted. My credits for graduation were very high, so I was not required to attend school but three days a week. I would go Mondays, Wednesdays, and Friday from eight in the mornings until twelve noon. That gave me the liberty to be home with my child, but at age seventeen, that was not my way of thinking. I knew my child was being well taken care of, so I took full advantage of my me time.

I would leave the house on the school bus and at twelve noon, I would go anywhere but home. My selfish, and self-willed way of doing things, led me down the road of rebellion. There was this fourteen-year old girl inside me crying out for help, but no one heard her cry. As a little girl, my granny Matilda would take me to church, and I would hear about God. I never understood what it was about. At home, granny would get on her knees and pray to God. I would get mad because her crying and talking would wake me up from sleeping. Thank you, Granny for your prayers.

I continued to be rebellious and do what I wanted. One day my mom told me that if I did not want the responsibility of my own child, I would need to take her to her daddy house to live. At seventeen, the only thing on my mind was me, me, and me. I packed my child a bag and my mom took me to drop her off at her dads. I didn't know what the conversation was between my mom and Anthony\s parents, but they kept her.

After two weeks of my child being gone, a feeling of shame came over me. I was being affected by the guilt of my selfish actions. To add to my shame, I consciously held a secret and it was now bothering me. My mom and I got in the car and drove to get my child. I was happy to see my little angel, but inwardly, I was angry. A very broken young girl is what I was.

CHAPTER 4

The Secret is Out

FOR A WHOLE year after my child was born, I hid the secret of knowing the father listed on her birth certificate was not her biological father. James, who lived in California, was the father of my child. James had shown no concern of being part of Faith's life, so I had told Anthony that he was the father of my child. Anthony was there when James wasn't and that eased my fear. I knew that his parents would be too, but it was time for me to come clean with the truth.

I called Anthony and asked him to come over so I could talk to him about something. When he arrived, I started a pleasant conversation with him to calm my nerves and prepare for his reaction. As I told Anthony the truth of Faith not being his child, the look on his face and in his eyes was heartbreaking. I was expecting him to hit me, but he didn't. I deserved to be hit by Anthony. He had provided for and loved my Faith and learning the truth devastated him.

Anthony did not accept the truth of what I told him. and left my house to tell his parents. He told his parents and they did not accept the truth either. As far as they were concerned, Faith was Anthony's daughter and their granddaughter, and it didn't matter what I had said. Finally, the truth was out. The guilt I no longer had to carry, but the shame of my actions I lived with daily.

Regardless of my self-willed, rebellious, stubborn, and hard-headed way of doing things, I could always depend on my mom. She tried to steer me into the right direction the best and only way she knew how. As days, weeks, and months passed on, the new year, 1982, was soon approaching. I would be turning eighteen in January and graduating from high school that May. I wore a smile on the outside but a very wounded and confused young girl on the inside.

I assume that my mom felt I needed something to help me become more responsible. She got me a job working with my sister, Alexa, at a pizza hut in one of the surrounding towns where we lived. I was making my own money and was totally opposite of responsible. I was selfish. I would get paid and go wherever I wanted and do whatever I wanted. I was a seven-teen year old trying to cope and exist as a normal adult woman. I had never been normal from my birth, and now I am a teenage mom at seventeen. What's normal about that?

CHAPTER 5

Dream Becomes Reality

I T WAS ON December 31, 1981 when I had a dream that was so surreal. In the dream, my mom dies in a tragic car accident. I wanted to tell someone about the dream, but I was afraid. Instead, I kept it to myself. For the next two weeks, I felt a small amount of anxiety, and the question that remained in my mind was "When is it going to happen?" I tried to focus on how I would celebrate my coming eighteenth birthday, but "When is it going to happen?" stayed in the fore front of my mind.

January 1982 came and on Thursday, January 14th, I turned eighteen years old. The next day, January 15th, my mom drove me to work. I worked my scheduled hours, my mom picked me up from work, and dropped me off at home. I did not see her again until the following Sunday evening. Hugs, kisses, and I love you was not the normal custom at my house. This day, January 17, 1982, I felt a desire to hug, kiss, and tell my mom that I loved her, but I didn't. I watched as she dressed in the mirror putting on her makeup. I asked her where she was going. She replied, "None of your business, I am grown." I couldn't take my eyes off my beautiful mom.

My mom finished getting dressed, walked out the door, and headed down the trail to my granny's house. I looked out the window and my eyes followed her as far as my poor eye sight would allow. When I couldn't see her any longer, I began to prepare for work. My sister, Alexa, picked me up. We put in our time and headed home. There was a song playing on the radio entitled, "A House is not a Home" The country was always dark, but as we topped a hill outside the limits of our town, my sister and I noticed there was a brightness in the sky ahead of us. I had brought my neighbor some food from my job and my sister drove me by her house to drop it off before we headed home. As the car came to a stop, there was a knock on the drives side window. My worst nightmare would soon be a reality.

As my sister rolled down the window, my brother in law said, "Your mom has been in a bad car accident." Time stood still and my mind went back to the dream I had On December 31, 1981. I opened my mouth and the words "She's dead, isn't she?" came out. Hesitantly, his reply was "Yes, she is." I could say that I was in dismay, but I wasn't. The words, "She's dead isn't she" would comfort my awaited expectancy. The words "Yes she is" would confirm my dream. I was shocked to the core of my soul and numb from the inside out. From that day forward, time would remain still for me.

My brother in law drove my sister and I to my granny's house. When I walked into the hose, my granny was crying but she appeared to be very calm. A pillow, and a pillar, is what my granny was for me that moment.

CHAPTER 6

Time Stands Still

AFTER BEING AT my grannies for a while, I called my daddy. I told him what had happened to my mom. I don't remember how old I was when I met my daddy because it was a secret. My mom had conceived me out of wedlock. As a child, I remember how my skin tome was much darker than my sisters and brother. I felt so ugly and different. When the truth came out about whose I was, and I met my daddy, he would come to visit me, and I would go to his house for visits. I loved my daddy.

When my daddy and his wife made it to my grannies, they took me and my child back to their house. Time is still for me and I feel like I am in a bubble. I remember just lying there in a very dark room waiting for the sun to rise. I was numb from the inside out. I kept telling myself that someone is going to call me and tell me that I imagine all this, but reality was reminding me that this was the expected end that I anxiously awaited.

The dark room brightened as the sun rose. I felt paralyzed but I managed to get dressed. My child and I were taken to a cousin's house to stay while my dad and step mom were at work. Tawanda didn't say much to me, but her presence made all the difference in the world. I couldn't cry, talk, or do anything but sit there silently in a chair. As I sit in that soft, cushioned chair, it seemed to caress me. I wanted my mom, but she wasn't coming back. Everyone that was around me treated me kindly and was very attentive, but no matter what anyone said or done, I was stuck in time inside a bubble.

I called Anthony and he picked me up and brought me to his parent's house. After all the pain I had put them through, they embraced me with open arms. The night before my mother's funeral, Anthony held me all night and I could feel the bubble burst. Tears began to flow from my eyes like a waterfall. I felt like my life was over the night my mom died and the day of her funeral, I wanted to be in the casket with her.

My mom's death was a shock, but I was expecting it. Strange, I know. The reality of it all set in when I walked into the church to a closed casket. Because my mom's body was so badly injured, there would be no open casket for final goodbyes. No hand to touch, no face to kiss. Nothing but a closed casket to look at. I cried so hard and don't remember anything but that closed casket sitting up front. My mom was gone, and I did not get the chance to tell her how much I loved her. I didn't get the chance to tell her how sorry I was for being such a disobedient child. I didn't get to tell her how sorry I was for causing her heart-ache and pain.

I grieved the loss of my mother, but the guilt and shame of how I disrespected and taken her for granted grieved me more. I had never felt so alone as I did on the day of my mom's funeral. I went to a friend's house after the service. I could see my house across the field. The house that I lived in with my mom, was now empty, dark, and cold. Days passed, but time stood still. I was alive, walking, talking, and breathing, but inside I was numb. I was numb to any feeling of worth, joy, or peace and felt nothing but regret, guilt, and shame.

CHAPTER 7

Why Me

I HADN'T RETURNED to my house since the day my mom died and did not want to. What would I do there? How would I live? Who was going to take care of me and my child now? I didn't know anything about being a grown up. My sister, Alexa and her family, decided to move into the house with me. The time had come for us to go back to the house. We needed to gather my mother's belongings. Her clothes, shoes, jewelry, under garments, everything she left behind.

Walking into that house would be one the hardest things to do. For a moment, I imagined walking inside and finding my mom there. As my sister and I entered the house, I felt unsettled. Each corner I turned, I expected to see my mom. I never saw her, but, the sweet scent of her aroma was everywhere. As I put each piece of clothing into a box, I was made aware of just how little I knew about her. I had been so focused on my own selfish ways, that I neglected to appreciate my mom. Closing those boxes, finalized her death in my mind. I felt hopeless and helpless.

The house was ready for my sister and her family to move in and they did. The place I called home, didn't feel like home anymore. My sister took the role of my mom and took care of my daughter and I. Going to school gave me a way of escape.

Escape from the misery I felt. I wanted to be anywhere but at my house.

High School graduation day had come. I had no feeling of joy, or excitement. I felt anger, bitterness, heartache, pain, loneliness, guilt and shame, and worthless. Most of my family members were there, but I didn't care. I wanted my mom. I watched as my classmates enjoyed their families. I needed to get away from that atmosphere. I went to turn in my cap and gown and as I walked down the dark side walk, it felt like I was in a dark tunnel. I remember being afraid, but not of the dark. I was afraid of the unknown. My senior graduation was supposed to be filled with beautiful memories, but this day would be one of my worst.

I went back to the gathering and wore a fake smile. My sister, Tiny, and my brother, Sidney were unable to attend my graduation. As a gift, they gave me a round trip ticket to visit them on the west coast. My daddy wanted me to visit him before I flew out, so I went to his house to stay for a couple of weeks. I was mentally and psychologically wounded. The thought of flying away from my surroundings that was causing me so much pain, gave me a small feeling of hope. I packed for me and my child and went to stay with my daddy.

I loved my daddy. In my eyes he was the smartest and strongest man in the world. When I was a little girl, spending time with him was my joy. I felt safe and secure like a little princess. He gave me the nickname bright eyes and maybe because my eyes were not so bright. I loved and respected my daddy. He was my hero. As time grew closer for my departure to the west coast, I asked my hero for money to take with me.

His reply to me was "If you help me out, I will help you." What could I help him do?" my hero was the strongest man in the world, he doesn't need any help from me. I am nothing or nobody. I asked him what he wanted me to help him do. He replied, "I will give you three hundred dollars for your trip if you help me out and let me sleep with you." I didn't think I could feel any lower than I felt at that very moment. The pain, emptiness, ugliness, sorrow, guilt and shame that I already felt, became so intense, I wanted to die again. That little broken girl inside me screamed even louder than she had before but still no one heard her.

What had I done or said to make him think I wanted him that way? I was his daughter that had shown nothing but genuine Love and respect for her daddy. I needed somebody I could talk to, but who? No one would believe me. My hero is well known in the community and very popular. Everybody respects him. I am nothing or nobody but a girl who got pregnant at sixteen with a baby. I told no one and convinced myself that my hero did not mean any of it. I waited for the day before I was to fly out, and I asked my hero again for help. I was expecting an apology for his hurting me. instead, His reply was the same. I was an emotional wreck. I covered my face and was introduced to prostitution and incest by my hero.

CHAPTER 8

Rescue Me

I FLEW OUT to the west coast where my brother, Sidney, picked me up from the air airport. I wore a smile to appear storing, happy, and stable for my child's sake. On the inside, I was broken, angry, guilty, ashamed, and filled with despair. I felt worthless and good for nothing. I was treated very well by my sister, brother, and their siblings. Their mother, Miss. Jewel, was one of the kindest persons and made me feel so wanted there in her home.

For two weeks, I seen and heard something in that house that I was not familiar with. People said "I love you" to one another. I felt out of place, yet welcome. I tried to be as pleasant and kind as I knew how to be. I wanted to do good and be good, but I didn't know how to be. My anger, pain, guilt, shame, and broken heart guided my choices. I did not know how to embrace the love and comfort that was being poured out on me. I began to feel a little bit of hope, but each time I thought of the return home, my mind shut all the good thoughts down.

I flew back and went to my hero's house. After being there for a few weeks that seemed life months, I met Sam. I was eighteen and Sam was twenty-five. He had his own house and asked me to move in with him. Sam was very kind to me and my child. I desperately needed and wanted to get out of my hero's house. Moving in with Sam would be my way of escape, so I did. Sam told me that he was a recovering alcoholic. I had been around alcohol, but I did not know what a recovering alcoholic was. Sam was a working man and took good care of me and my child. I later found out that Sam had issues too.

One evening Sam and I were conversating and he began to accuse me of being unfaithful. I tried to reassure him that I was not. Sam got so upset that he stuck his cigarette to my leg. I still have the burn mark today. What did I say or do to upset him? I didn't understand his actions. "Oh well", I thought, "he won't do it again." I stayed with him. What else was I to do?

The next morning, nothing was said about the night before. Sam left for work and I started breakfast. I was cooking when one of my cousins stopped by to say hello. I invited him to stay for breakfast and he accepted. We were eating and laughing, and just having fun, when Sam walked into the house. I introduced my cousin to Sam as he walked past us to the back of the house. My cousin said "Well, I'm going to go." We were enjoying each other so I didn't know why he felt the need to leave. I walked him out and came back in to the house.

Sam came into the front and began telling me how he didn't want any man in his house while he wasn't at home. I tried to tell Sam that I hadn't done anything wrong. Before I could say another word, Sam hit me so hard that my head bounced off the inside kitchen doorway. I saw stars floating around in darkness, and nearly blacked out. I stayed on my feet somehow. I felt I needed to get out of that house. When

Sam walked to the back of the house, I grabbed up my child, and ran out the door. Thankfully, there was a police officer right across the street. I called my sister Alexa and asked if I could move in with her and her family and she said yes. My sister picked me up and I moved in.

Moving back into the house that I had once shared with my mom, was a daily reminder of how I had taken her for granted. I would lie in bed at night and look for my mom to come to me. I wanted so bad to see her so I could talk to her and tell her how sorry I was. I wanted to tell her everything that had happened to me. I wanted my mom

My mind was loaded with the guilt, and shame from the things I had done. Nothing good happened for me and I was to blame for all the bad. I was good for nothing and saw no good in anything. I was a very miserable and horrible person. Anthony would come around and visit from time to time and even he didn't realize how troubled I was, but he later found out. My rebellious actions were so horrid that my granny thought I was possessed with an evil spirit.

On one occasion, Anthony held me, while my granny tried to beat the devil out of me. My brother in law, David could see that I was spiraling and needed help and he asked me to attend church with him. I declined his first invitation, but he didn't stop asking.

CHAPTER 9

Accepted and Rejected

I FELT I had nothing to live for. My mind was entangled by pain, guilt, shame, anger, and regret. The clock of time in my mind had not moved since the day of my mom's death. I wasn't living life, but life was living me. I was deep in depression with no sign of hope. My brother in law David was not giving up on me and invited me to church again. I accepted his invitation and went with him to church.

It was on a Wednesday, January 19, 1983. when I went to church with my brother in law. This church was different from the one I had attended as a child with my granny. It was vibrant and loud. The pastor asked if anyone wanted to be baptized. I sat there for a minute trying to understand what it meant to be baptized. I decided to go up front. When I got up there, I began to cry. People began to pray for me and tell me to say Thank you Jesus repetitively. I was so confused and didn't know what to do but obey them. After a while of repeating Thank you Jesus, I wanted to stop, but they kept saying "Let him change it" Who was him and what was he going to change? I started screaming, shouting, and jumping around.

I had heard about how people jump and shout at this church, so I guess I was experiencing it. I was told to come back on the next Friday so I could get baptized and tarry for the Holy Ghost. I was even more confused because I thought screaming, yelling, and jumping, was the Holy Ghost. Whatever it was, it made me feel better. I didn't know what tarry meant, but I learned about it. After I got baptized, I was taken to the alter and was told to repeatedly say "Thank you Jesus" I was what they called tarrying. I did this for a while and my speech changed to something I didn't understand. I finally stopped speaking. I was asked "What happened to you?" I said, "I think I got the Holy Ghost." I wasn't sure of what happened to me. I had seen people do this and called it the Holy Ghost, so I assumed I had it. All I knew was that for the first time in over a year, time began to move again.

Singing was my passion, so I joined the choir and became very active in the church. I was being taught about the God that would send you to hell for committing fornication, adultery, drinking, smoking, stealing, lying, cursing, and murder. Hell, fire, and damnation was taught vigorously. I was learning how to be very religious and righteous and it felt good, but I was still set in my way of doing things and that was not good. Something was missing.

Summer was here and James came down from California. I started spending time with him and got pregnant again. This time it was on me because I knew better but chose to do it anyway. When my pastor found out I was pregnant, he sat me down out the choir and I was unable to participate in any church activities. Being an unmarried pregnant mother was unacceptable and there were consequences behind my actions.

I was still living with my sister and her family. When I told my sister I was pregnant, she said I would have to move out. I was nineteen with one child and pregnant with my second child. I didn't know where I would go but my granny told me

I could live with her. I moved in with my granny and went to church faithfully. I was happy living with my granny. Even though I couldn't participate in church, I was content in just going. Knowing that I would be back in the choir once I had my child, kept my hope alive.

On April 8, 1984, I came into labor around six o'clock that morning, got dressed, and went to church. Later that evening my water began to leak so I called mother Angel and Bonnie to come drive me to the hospital. On our way there, the car ran out of gas. I had been in labor for about eighteen hours already. I was scared and crying out in pain. I could feel my child getting ready to come out. Thankfully, Bonnie walked to a nearby house and called my brother in law David. He came, picked us up, and drove us to the hospital. Thirty minutes after my arrival, I gave natural birth to a seven-pound baby boy.

I was twenty years old and a single mother of two kids. Going to church and hearing about God made me feel good. Still, there was a void inside me.

CHAPTER 10

On My Own

MY GRANNY TALKED to me about moving into my own house and the responsibilities of it all. The thought of being on my own sounded exciting, but scary. Taking on that kind of responsibility seemed impossible for me. I had nothing but my two kids. I don't know if it was my mom, sister, or granny that put me on state assistance {welfare}, but my granny told me about it and how much I would get. Within a few months of having my son, at the age of twenty, I moved into my own little house with my two kids.

For the first time, I felt like a grown up, or at least what I thought it felt like to be grown. Because of my visual impairment, I didn't drive so I had no drivers license. Granny or my sister would drive me where I needed to go. I was receiving two hundred eighteen dollars in cash and two hundred ninety-two dollars in food stamps per month. On the first of each month, I would pay my bills, buy groceries, and purchase what I needed for my house with whatever was left. it was very hard making ends meet, and I did whatever needed to be done to take care of my kids.

Being introduced to prostitution would be my way of making extra money. When I couldn't get money form anyone or anyplace else, I would call my hero and ask him for help.

I longed for the day to come when I could call him and hear him say "Daddy love you and I'm on my way." Instead, he would always say "I need help too." I would threaten to tell his actions toward me, but he would say "Who's going to believe you over me?" Psychologically that little girl, believed the words of her hero.

Going to church inspired the outer me. Inwardly, I struggled daily with myself and the feelings of my insecurities. Anger, grief, sorrow, sexual, mental, emotional and psychological abuse, were issues not addressed or elaborated on in my church. All the issues that I carried daily. I smiled, and tried to walk the righteous walk, but I was broken, bruised, and void of understanding. There was still something missing in my life, but what it was, I didn't know.

On April 20, 1984, I met a tender-hearted man named Wilson. Wilson was hard working and helped me in every way he could. He and I started a relationship and became a couple. The void I felt, seemed to be comforted by Wilson's presence, but it was still there. I attended church regularly, but Wilson, did not go to church. I wanted to get married, but he was not ready for marriage. I told Wilson we should get married so we wouldn't be fornicating and if he didn't marry me, I would find someone else. On June 30, 1986, Wilson became my first husband.

SIMPLY TRUTH

CHAPTER 11

My First Husband

THE DAY I married Wilson, was one of my happier days. It was a day that I did not focus on any of my issues. I focused on being a good wife to Wilson. I was twenty-two years old when Wilson and I got married. Physically, I was trying to do the right thing, but spiritually, I was in desperate need of understanding. I needed to understand why I felt and acted the way I did, and what I needed to change.

This was Wilson's first marriage too. I loved Wilson the best way I knew how to love him. My insecurities didn't make it easy for him to love me, but he did the best he could. How could I love someone when I didn't know how to love myself? My daughter was three and my son eleven days old when Wilson and I met. He was so good to my children.

On May 17, 1987, God blessed Wilson and I with our first child together. Wilson was so excited and happy to see his newborn daughter. She was the joy of his life. I wanted to have Wilson a son, but he said he did not feel the need for any more children. I listened to what he said, but I was determined to give him a boy. On October 11, 1988, the same day of my mom's birthday, we gave birth to a baby boy. Wilson was so proud of his children because there was a time in his life where he didn't think he could have any. I had two children when Wilson and I met, and he was the only man they knew as daddy. Now we had four beautiful children.

Wilson eventually joined the church and we went attended together. I had my own family going to church, but I carried around so much baggage. How could I completely be happy and free knowing I was full of unhealthy issues and secrets. I could feel God loving me as I was, but I needed to learn about the love of God.

SIMPLY TRUTH

CHAPTER 12

I Will Trust you

FOR YEARS, I was living with a guilty conscience bought on by my own will and the mental, emotional, psychological, and physical abuse of others. I was familiar with prayer, but I didn't feel the need to get serious about it. At times, I would wake up in the middle of the night and something would tell me to pray. I started praying daily. There was something different going on inside me. Something good was happening to me.

The more I prayed, the more I became aware of the inner me. I was learning that I needed to open my heart to God for change to take place inside me. Opening my heart would be a challenge because it required trust. Trust had caused me so much pain. Pain that I was still carrying around in my heart. I needed to be set free from this pain. Loving God and trusting him would be the start of loving myself.

Of all the pain I carried, the worst of it all was the painful secret of what I endured from my hero. The secret that God knew about all the time. The thought of being set free from that burden gave me a feeling of peace. At the same time, the thought of peace was shortened by the shame of it. I was now starting to hear my spirit conscience and it said to trust God. I had waited years for someone to rescue me by asking "Is he bothering you?" no one ever asked me. Now I'm hearing this sweet quiet voice saying "Trust Me" it was time for me to tell my secret to someone, but who. I called the only person that came to my mind. I called my pastor and told him I needed to talk to him.

We met at the church to talk, I couldn't say a word. Tears flowed from my eyes and heart. God prepared my pastor before he came because he knew all that I would say even before I said it. I didn't feel judged, but I felt shame. God proved himself to be trustworthy and I could feel His loving arms around me. No more secrets, no more lies. Free at last free at last Thank God I was free at last.

I was on the road to recovery. Recovery from the bondage of guilt, shame, and regret. It felt good, but I had a long way to go. I was free from the burden and ready to learn about and receive Gods love. I loved, but my way of loving came from a place of brokenness. I was feeling more hopeful than I had felt. My life and my future were looking brighter.

A few weeks after revealing the secret I went to a women's retreat for the weekend. The main topic that the speakers spoke on was "Gods Love". it amazed me how God knew what I needed and met me where I was. I remember being called out of the audience to tell what I had learned there. I don't' remember exactly what I said but I do remember something inside of me shifted. My shift was very noticeable to my children because they told me that I was acting different. I knew I had ugly ways and not so kind. Seeing my children notice the good change in me, made me realize how broken I was and how it had hurt them.

CHAPTER 13

The Curve Ball

THINGS WERE GOING well for my family, but we needed a second income. One day I was in a store and saw these clip-on sunglasses that fit over prescription glasses. I got a pair and was so happy because they helped me to see better. Wilson encouraged me to learn how to drive and taught me. At age twenty-five, I took the test. The instructor said, "I'm going to give you a license, but you need to see your eye doctor." I knew it was God that favored me to get my license. I applied for a job and got it. Driving to and from work was very strenuous but I did what needed to be done. I trusted God, and I drove

Wilson and I stopped going to church and fellowshipping with other believers. Making that move was not a good choice for either of us. Our marriage wasn't as pleasant as it had been and was suffering because of our actions. Thankfully, no matter what the situation was and through our unfaithfulness to one another, we never separated. We stayed together. I was injured on my job and could not perform the required duties. I was no longer employed there, but the employer payed for me to attend a vocational school for rehabilitation. I stated training for Business and Computer Technology and attend school five days a week.

Wilson and I needed to get back in fellowship with God and other believers and we did. Wilson started a new job at the previous place I had worked. I knew the environment, and it wasn't good. My husband worked the evening shift and on Sundays. The absence of bible study and fellowship was spiritually unhealthy for my husband. I noticed a change in Wilson, and felt distance between us. I asked him what was bothering him, and he told me he wasn't happy.

I had this uneasy feeling that something was not right and that it involved a woman. I told Wilson that if he wasn't happy, he should do what was needed to be happy. I was referring to getting more involved with church. Wilson knew that was the right thing to do, but he decided to go to the left. Wilson left me and the kids. I was dazed, but not surprised. My heart was broken once again.

I was at a loss and didn't know which way to go from there. I remained faithful to my church attendance, but my feelings were all over the place and I focused on my problems. Dwelling on my pain took my mind down the memory lane of my past and God was no longer the center of my joy I wanted Wilson to hurt like I hurt. My anger, bitterness, and vengeful thoughts took center stage in my mind.

The pain of Wilson leaving was awful, and I didn't know how I would make it through. Continual bible study and fellowship eliminated my thoughts of revenge, but I struggled with anger, bitterness, and unforgiveness. My spirit conscience pointed me to the book of Job from the bible. I would read that book daily and it strengthened me. Wilson had been gone for a while when I started hearing bits and pieces about a woman. The woman was allegedly the one he left me for. I wanted to know the truth.

It was my oldest daughter's junior prom. Faith asked Wilson if she could drive his truck to the prom and he said yes. When Wilson pulled up in the driveway to drop off the truck, a woman pulled up behind him in a separate car. When I saw her, I knew she was the one he left me for. I felt my temper rising and wanted to shoot them. Instead, my spirit conscience said, "Be nice." I walked over to her car, said hello, and invited them in. She declined and they left.

Wilson leaving me affected me more than I expected. I was not going to subject myself to that kind of disrespect. He was being unfaithful so I divorced him in hope that it would sooth my hurt and pain. I wanted to feel better, but I didn't

CHAPTER 14

My Provider and Protector

BEING A SINGLE mom again was the last thing I ever expected but this time it was different. I knew about God and was learning to trust him. Anger, bitterness, and unforgiveness clouded my mind and now my insecurities had popped its ugly head back up. "She must have been prettier than me, smarter than me, better than me." I tried to figure it out and the more I tried, the angrier I got.

I was still attending vocational school. Wilson had been my main source of income and he was gone. One of the requirements for my studies was to do a two week on the job training as a part of my grade. The school sent me to a telephone company to do the training. I needed a paying job to provide for my children. I spoke to the president of the company and told him about my situation. I was hired that day as the receptionist. I quit vocational school and began working full time.

I was making three hundred and fifty dollars every two weeks with four children. How was I going to make it on this little bit of money? Wilson payed three hundred dollars a month in child support and I used that to make my car payment. I wanted many times to just give up, but I thought about my children. I could have applied for food stamps to help buy food, but I didn't think about it because I was getting commodities through the Chickasaw Nation. Every month I would pick the food up and that's what my kids and I survived on. I wasn't financially able to give my children the things they wanted, but not once did my kids go hungry, without water, lights, shoes, clothes, or any necessity, and I always had gas to get to and from work.

I really liked my job, but I did not enjoy having to drive there or back. I was facing the rising sun on the way to work and facing the setting sun on the way home. I drove in fear each day I went to work and home from work. I would pray "God, please protect me and anyone in my way." I was driving home one day facing the sun. I could feel my car driving over the train tracks, but I did not see the train coming. I heard the train whistle blowing but wasn't aware of the danger I was in until the guard rail hit my windshield. My windshield was shattered on the passenger side, but it didn't fall out. Buy the grace of God, I made it safely home that day and every day. I would not let anyone other than my children ride with me unless it was necessary. Given the choice, my children would have chosen not to ride with me. I would have chosen not to ride with myself.

CHAPTER 15

My Second Husband

I WAS STILL faithfully attending bible study, singing in the choir, and participating in church activities. Wilson would come by and visit the kids and take them for weekend visits. One night he came to the house and told me he was getting married. He did not appear to be a happy and excited man. I still loved Wilson and was not pleased to hear his news.

My dad had joined the church and our relationship was wonderful. My kids and I were visiting him one day when I met this younger man named Rodney. I was single in status, but very much emotionally broken. I still had many issues going on inside me. I didn't think about being with man when I was alone, but around Rodney, my flesh was screaming, and I wanted to answer the call.

Being the religious woman that I was, I told Rodney I would not sleep with him unwed. Two weeks after meeting him, we got married. Once again, I was set down at church and was not allowed to participate in any church activities. I was upset and not pleased about it. I married Rodney to keep from fornication, but I knew my reasoning wasn't right. Rodney didn't understand why I was set down and I tried to explain to him the ways of my church. He hung in there with me for thirty days and then left me and the church. I divorced him and was allowed back in the choir and carried on with church activities.

Divorcing Rodney was painful, but it was no pain compared to the pain I felt when I divorced Wilson. It was right before Christmas when I received the finalized divorce papers for Rodney. I was having a pity party, and Wilson called to ask if he could have the kids for the holiday. In a way, his request would be for the best because I had nothing but twenty dollars to buy my children Christmas gifts. At least being with Wilson for the holidays, they would have a good Christmas.

I went to the dollar general store and bought socks and a few VCR tapes and wrapped it for my children to have gifts from their momma when they came home. This was the first Christmas I spent alone without my children. I cried because I was alone, but more from the thought of not being able to get my children what they asked for. Knowing they were with Wilson and having a good Christmas gave me comfort.

CHAPTER 16

My Third Husband

WILSON WOULD COME by the house from time to time and pick up the kids. We would conversate about what was going on in our lives. He told me he and his wife had divorced. I was still holding on to the pain of him leaving me, so I was happy to hear about his divorce. I still loved Wilson, but I was angry, and unforgiving about what he had done to me.

Wilson continued coming around and we began to bond again. A few months passed and we decided to get married again to keep from fornicating. I knew Wilson cared for me and me for him. None the less, we both had our own issues and needed to be healed from our brokenness. We needed to be Spiritually whole and healthy for ourselves and our children. Life continued with me being my self-righteous and self-willed way and Wilson being his way.

We were together for about six months when Wilson started acting distant again. I knew this familiar pattern. He would be late coming home from work and said he was working overtime. I knew in my heart what it was, but I wanted him to tell me. I wanted him to tell me there was someone else and not let me here it from the streets.

I was sitting at work and Wilson called me. He said "I am leaving" I got so nervous and upset I left work and came home. When I go there, he was packing and getting ready to leave. I took his keys and said to him "You are not going anywhere until the kids come home from school. You will be the one to tell them, not me." He wasn't happy about that, but I didn't care. When the kids came home, he told them.

I will never forget how our baby daughter begged her daddy to stay. She cried so hard and that infuriated me. I was more angered about him hurting our kids than I was about him hurting me. I thought that maybe he would stay after he saw his daughter begging and crying, but he left anyway. I was so angry with Wilson and blaming him that I failed to see that I was hurting the children just as much as he was. I wasted no time and divorced Wilson. Didn't talk to God about it, just did what I wanted to do. Wilson had hurt me for the last time. The reality was the fact that I was hurting myself by following my self-willed and self-righteous ways.

I didn't stop going to church, but still no relationship with God. I wasn't ready to give up my way of doing things. Years of hearing about God, but I still didn't know Him. I knew the ten commandments, but that wasn't all to be learned about God and His Word. I had religion, and followed the traditions, but I had no personal relationship with God. I was growing in some areas of my life, but I needed a complete transformation of my heart.

One day Anthony showed up at my house. He was looking good and smelling good too. We chatted a while and caught up on what we had been doing with ourselves. Anthony and I were not intimate but on this one evening, he tried to kiss me. I kissed him but then I pulled away and told him NO, I was not going down that road. I felt a strength in me that I hadn't felt before. My low self-esteem was being changed and strengthened to a level of self-worth.

CHAPTER 17

My Fourth Husband

I WAS FEELING a different kind of me, but I knew there had to be more. I was still working as a receptionist and was fired from my job. It was one of those incidents where I got blamed for something I did not do. I was ready to hire a lawyer and dispute, but my spirit conscience said, "Let it go." I wasn't off work for very long when I got a part time job at the local post office right down the street from my house.

Wilson had a girlfriend, and they had broken up. We started hanging out again. I felt sorry for Wilson because he did not have a place to sleep so I allowed him to sleep in one of my spare bedrooms. I told him that he could not stay there too long because it didn't look right for us to be sharing a house. I still had feelings for Wilson, and there were a few times when the flesh got weak, but my desire for a man had changed.

I was growing spiritually, but still felt a void inside. Wilson stayed in the spare bedroom for a while. Financially, he was a blessing to me and giving him a place to stay was a blessing for him. It was convenient for the both of us. Wilson wanted physical intimacy, but he knew how I felt about fornication. He asked me to marry him. I knew this was not right because of the reason why he wanted to marry me. Our two oldest children had graduated high school and gone. Our younger children were still at home, so I used that as a reason to marry Wilson. I looked past the wrong in my decision to marry him, and I made the choice to use convenience as a right to do it.

There were several incidents that reminded me of why I shouldn't marry Wilson, but I did it anyway. This would be my third time marrying him. I didn't desire Wilson and I knew it. I did not trust him and had plenty of reasons not to. I kept myself busy to keep my mind occupied. It didn't take long for Wilson to get restless again. I wasn't satisfied with Wilson either because I wasn't satisfied with myself.

Anthony was in prison and sent a message to ask if I would write him. I asked Wilson if it would be ok if I correspond with Anthony, and he said yes. I thought that was very abnormal for my husband to give me permission to write my ex-boyfriend. That familiar uneasy feeling about Wilson came over me again. I knew it was another woman somewhere. I went to bible study one night and my daughter said a woman had called the house for Wilson. I got the number off my caller id and looked up a name to match.

I was talking with a friend one day and she asked me if I knew a certain person. She called the name out and it was the name of the person on my caller id. My friend worked at the same place my husband worked and told me that Wilson was having an affair with the woman. I began to put all the puzzle pieces together and they fit. There were many other signs that followed leading to his unfaithfulness. I wasn't surprised at any of it. I would ask Wilson about the things I heard, but he would always deny it. It didn't matter his denial because the truth always came to me.

Writing Anthony helped to keep my mind off what was going on in front of me. I knew writing Anthony while married to Wilson was not the right thing for me to be, but I did it anyway. I told Wilson he needed to leave. The other times, he left me, but this time, I was putting him out. We stayed separated for a while and I even considered getting back together with him. Each time I would be somewhere with Wilson, he would get suspicious phone calls from females. Wilson would not talk on the phone in my presence but would walk away to talk. I divorced Wilson and continued writing Anthony.

CHAPTER 18

My Fifth Husband

I HAD GOTTEN married four times and three of those times to the same man. You would have thought that I was tired and ready to do it Gods way, but I wasn't. Single I was again in status but still emotionally broken. My fortieth birthday was coming up and I was ready to celebrate it. I felt a more secure and content me, but that void inside was still there.

All my children had left home except for my youngest son and a nephew who was living with me. The boys were good and gave me no trouble. I was still writing Anthony and at times he would call me from prison. My son did not like my choice of writing or talking with Anthony. I didn't see any harm writing a man locked up in prison. In one of Anthony\s letters he told me that he was coming up for a parole hearing. I was happy for Anthony and hoped he got paroled.

I was growing into a woman that no longer felt the need for a man to take care of me. I was taking care of myself and the boys and was satisfied without a man in my life. When I did think of having someone special, I thought companionship. Intimacy would be good, but it wasn't a necessity. I was just glad to be loving myself for the first time and learning to live alone. I wasn't dating anyone and had no desire to. Writing Anthony was good enough for me.

However, the more we wrote, the closer we became. The letters were innocent at first, but the conversations got passionate and personal. I should have been focusing on learning how to surrender and submit to God. instead, I was lusting after Anthony. As usual, the big "M" word came into our conversation. We decided we would get married if he got released on parole. The months to come would be wavering for me. I knew in my mind I was moving too fast.

Anthony was released from prison and we were married two days later. He had nothing when he got out but the clothes on his back, his shoes, and a few dollars. I knew what I was getting myself into in reference to supporting him until he could support himself. I didn't marry him for material things, I married him because of lust. Wrong reason to marry anybody.

When my pastor found out that I had married Anthony, I was once again set down from participating in any church activities. My pastor believed that Anthony and I were unequally yoked. The place of worship that I attended at the time believed that if a person was not baptized in the name of Jesus and filled with the Holy Ghost with the evidence of speaking in tongues (Acts 2:38), that person was not a believer, not saved, and going to hell.

Anthony had been baptized once in 1983 along with me. To please my pastor and some of the church members, he got baptized again. After a while, I was released to resumed church activities. As far as I was concerned, I was no more of a believer than Anthony was. I felt like an outcast in my church. without emotional or spiritual support. I was angry and bitter, but I didn't stop going. I could see Anthony's frustration, but he didn't stop going either. Anthony became an ordained minister and began preaching the gospel.

CHAPTER 19

Bitter Sweet

ANTHONY WAS NOT a lazy man and believed in working. We needed to focus on getting his driver license reinstated. In the meantime, he went to work on a nearby farm to help with financial obligations. I was still working at the post office. My income would carry us until he could get a license and a better job. We seemed to be on the right path.

My job was within walking distance from my home, so I didn't do much driving at all. Anthony was required by law to take DUI classed before he could be reinstated and take the exam for his license. The classes would take six weeks to complete and were being held in a town forty—five miles from our house. Three day a week, I would be the designated driver to and from the classes. Driving was not a pleasure for me, it was a tedious struggle.

Each evening while Anthony was in class, I would sit outside in the car and wait for him. There were times when I would sit for an hour or longer. I did my best when driving, but he did not like it. I wanted to quit many times in those six weeks, but I knew he needed my help. Oh, the joy and relief I felt when Anthony completed that class. I endured six weeks of torment. He tested for the exam, passed, and got his license. I was so proud of him.

Anthony got a very good job and purchased himself a nice truck. He was on a role doing very well and was determined to stay on the right path. Anthony and I continued going to our place of worship. The first two years of our marriage was sweet and pleasant. Low self-esteem was no longer an issue for me, bu Anthony struggled in that area. I appreciated Anthony and respected his position as my husband. Nevertheless, he treated me as if I was still his fourteen-year-old girlfriend. There were times when he tried to push me around, but I let him know that I was not afraid of him.

My son Junior, and nephew, Roland, decided to disobey me and sneak to a new-years-eve party. When I found out about it, my self-righteous mind kicked in and I sent them to live with Juniors father, Wilson. I was surprised at their actions because they had never given me any trouble before. Roland wanted to move back home, and I allowed him to. Junior was pleased to stay with his father because he was not fond of Anthony. Roland was a gentle and meek young mand and he and Anthony had no problems with one another. Anthony was a bit egotistical and arrogant. Roland knew it, but he admired and respected Anthony.

One evening we all decided to go to a football game. Roland wanted to ride home from the game with his friends. My self-righteous way of thinking did not see that as a good idea, so I said no. Roland was not happy with my answer and he began to murmur while sitting in the back seat. I had the situation under control, but Anthony being his arrogant, egotistical, and controlling self, stepped in. We had pulled into our driveway when Anthony and Roland began to confront one another. I didn't hear what Roland said to Anthony, but he was livid.

Before I could intervene, Anthony had grabbed Roland around his neck and threw him up against a wall. Anthony being six feet three inch grown man, and Roland a five-feet, five-inch kid, there was not much Roland could do. I yelled "Stop it! Stop it!" and attempted to break the hold that Anthony had on Roland. It seemed like forever, but Anthony released Roland and walked away. What could Roland have possibly said to Anthony to make him react with such rage?

To see Anthony's anger was familiar and disappointing, but to see Roland crying was upsetting for me. Roland was so angry and gripped his fist as he paced across the kitchen floor. Anthony stood there watching Roland and said, "Either he moves out or I'm moving out." I said "Well, Roland isn't going anywhere." Anthony looked at me, grabbed his keys, and left.

My only concern was comforting Roland. I asked Roland what he had said to make Anthony so angry. Roland explained to me that he told Anthony he was not a little boy nor his son. He was tired of Anthony\s arrogance and egotistical ways. Roland speaking his mind was a blow to Anthony's ego and hit an open soar. Anthony had four children that he did not have a relationship with because he chose to do his own thing. His choices had led him away from being a father to his children.

Anthony tried to fill the shoes as Roland's father and did not know how. Roland was not a little boy, but a gentle and respectable young man. He needed a role model, not an iron fist. Roland did not feel comfortable staying at home, so I allowed him to sleep at his aunties for the night. I was still in awe of what had happened

When Anthony came home, he walked into the house and asked where Roland was. I told him Roland would be staying the night at auntie Sally's. Anthony said, "So you not putting him out." I said, 'No I am not' Anthony said, "You must be sleeping with him." I was sick to my stomach and felt very nauseated hearing his sickening words.

In Anthony's distorted, twisted, and insecure way of thinking, I had chosen another man over him. I wanted to put Anthony out that night, but I didn't. Roland graduated high school and moved out. Things would not be the same between Anthony and me.

CHAPTER 20

There is Hope

I WAS HURT and angry on top of hurt and ager. Emotionally, I felt myself going into a me, myself, and I mind set, and I knew that was not good. I worked in the church diligently, but I needed to be delivered from my self-willed self-righteous ways. I needed to focus on my weaknesses, but it was easier for me to focus on Anthony's.

I could tell that Anthony was missing Roland's absence because he began talking about his children. Anthony told me that he had been asking God to open the door of communication between him and his kids. I wanted that for him and hoped it would happen. I understood that Anthony could not make up for the lost time, but given the opportunity, they could make a new start.

One evening Anthony and I were talking when his phone rang. He answered the phone and I could tell it was good news by his joyful expressions from the conversation. I didn't need to ask him who it was because I heard him call his daughters name. God had answered Anthony's prayer. Hope, Anthony's baby daughter was reaching out to her daddy. I was so happy for Anthony. Having my children and grandchildren in my life, was a beautiful feeling and I wanted Anthony to experience it as well. Anthony hadn't seen his daughter since she was a toddler. Hope's mother had come for a family visit to a nearby town from where we lived.

Anthony and Hope would talk daily on the phone. He made plans for his daughter to come for a weekend visit. We drove to pick her up and she appeared to very quiet and well behaved. As time passed, I could see that Hope was not as quiet as she appeared. She was a fourteen-year old girl that had her own way of thinking and doing things. Anthony couldn't see what I saw in her. One Friday evening, Anthony received a phone call from Hope's mother. She had taken the kids on a camping trip and Hope was being disrespectful and unruly. Hope's mom asked Anthony if he could come pick Hope up.

My spirit conscience told me then that Hope would be coming to live with us. It was confirmed a few weeks later when her mother asked Anthony if Hope could live with us. We decided we would get her. Anthony and I discussed what needed to be done. I told Anthony that we needed to be in agreeance and stick together in decision making for Hope. I reminded Anthony that Hope was not a baby anymore but a teen-age girl with her own personality.

Hope was fourteen when she moved in with us. Anthony was so excited to be given the chance to raise his daughter. What he failed to realize is that she was not that toddler he left behind. Things were going well at the beginning until we were faced with the decision of how to discipline Hope. Raising my children, I was very stern and unwavering. This would be Anthony's first chance to be a father to his child and he didn't want to do anything to anger Hope. He didn't want to say no to anything she wanted. My self-righteous way of doings things, and him with his egotistical way would add to the challenging task ahead.

Anthony and Hope formed a beautiful bond. They were like best friends which I loved to see that. Unfortunately, Anthony did not understand the difference between being a parent and a friend to his child. Hope was very self-willed. It was apparent that she was used to having things her way. Anthony either couldn't see or chose to ignore Hopes disrespectful and disobedient ways toward him. To see her treat him the way she did, bothered me. I would bring it to his attention, but he didn't want to acknowledge it. Anthony didn't mind me correcting Hope, but it had to be done his way.

Hope never disrespected me, and to see the pure love that Anthony had for his daughter was so very beautiful to me. Anthony and I were growing even farther apart. We attended church as a happy and united family, but at home we were divided. I became even more angry, bitter, and unforgiving.

CHAPTER 21

Get Out

BEING AROUND HOPE was like looking in a mirror at myself when I was her age. Angry, Rebellious, manipulative, stubborn, and very self-willed. I was grown now, and still carried some of these characteristics. I was so geared on pointing out Anthony and Hopes faults that I failed to see my own. Instead of griping and complaining, I should have been praying. Anthony and I were emotionally, physically, and spiritually unattached and it hurt. Staying in the me, myself, and I mode, made it easier for me to not care about anything going on around me.

Hope and Anthony were in the kitchen talking. As I walked in, I heard Hope say, "I'm going to tell on you.' I said, "Tell what?" Anthony quickly said." You better not." Hope said, "My daddy is watching porno and he said he is not happy making love with you." Did that child say what I think I heard her say? was so embarrassed. I looked at Anthony and he had this look of guilt on his face and he grinned. I turned and walked out the kitchen.

As days passed, I chose to shut down my compassion towards either of them. I felt the safest place for me was in my own arms. No one could hurt me there. Anthony would try to talk to me and explain why he had said what he did, but it didn't matter to me his reason, the damage was done. I had lusted after this man and now he doesn't want me. My self-esteem reverted backwards, and I sulked in my own self-pity.

Why do I need to stay with him? if he's watching porno, that means he is being unfaithful. I was not pleased with Anthony at all. I allowed my pride, bitterness, anger, and unforgiveness sway me into telling Anthony he had to leave my house. I never took into consideration how my actions would affect anyone. I wanted the pain to go away and this was the way to do it.

Anthony tried to talk me out of my decision, but I didn't want to hear anything he had to say. My mind was made up and he had to go. Anthony packed what little he had and moved out with Hope. They moved into a house down the street but would come visit from time to time. I had made a very unthought out decision based off my hurt feelings and I felt bad about it. I lived with regret for months. Anthony nor Hope deserved to be the target of my self-made problem.

Self-righteously, I continued faithfully attending church. Anthony and Hope were still coming too. The sad part about my life was the fact that I was in church, but the church was not in me. I still hadn't surrendered my heart to God. The wall of my insecurities had been broken, but I chose to hold on to some of the pieces. I missed Anthony very much and I asked him to move back in so we could try to save our marriage. He agreed. After six months of separation, Anthony and Hope moved back into the house with me. There was something different about Anthony, and the bond that the he and Hope shared wasn't the same.

One morning, Anthony left for work, and Hope left for school. I was off work that day and was cleaning the house. I noticed a folded piece of paper on the kitchen countertop and I opened it. It was a note that Hope had written me. In the note, she told me that she loved me, but she didn't understand how I could go to church and be a Christian, yet, act and talk so mean and ugly. I found myself getting annoyed as I read the letter. Everything Hope said in her note was the truth about me.

Hope had been watching the life I lived. Inside the church walls, I was a faithful Christian working diligently. Outside the walls, I was a self-righteous hypocrite. This fifteen-year old child gave me a piece of her mind, and it irritated me. I read the note, several times over and found myself crying. The truth of Hopes words reproved my wrong and made me sorrowful.

Hope came home from school, hurried to her room, and closed the door. I knocked on the door and went in. The look on her face and the fear in her eyes made me so ashamed. I sat on the bed and looked her in the face. I said "Hope, I am so very sorry. Please forgive me." She said the same to me, we hugged, and made an agreement that in the future we would talk to each other about anything. I felt so relieved and she did too. I thought Anthony would be pleased with the bond that Hope and I formed, but he wasn't. He said mean things to make me look bad in front of her. Things between Hope and I were great, but the connection between Anthony and I was lost.

CHAPTER 22

The Angry Side

ANTHONY AND I were acting like strangers but Hope and I were loving and enjoying one another. I noticed Anthony starting to act strange and I felt he was drinking again. I knew he hadn't forgiven me for asking him to leave, but it was something else going on with him. I was ready and willing to put the pain of our past behind us, but I could tell that Anthony did not feel the same.

Anthony was so cold towards me. I could see the anger and resentment in his eyes when he looked at me. I hurt him very badly by my selfish actions. I accepted my faults in our marriage, but Anthony didn't see anything he had done or was doing wrong. Our marriage continued to go down-hill and it saddened me. I did not want to live this way. I would much rather be alone than with someone that despised me.

I told Anthony that I felt we should go our separate way, but Hope could stay. Hope felt she needed to take care of her daddy and told me she would go with him. Anthony didn't like it and said he wasn't going anywhere. I called the police and told them I wanted him to go. Anthony took everything he could including our bedroom furniture. I didn't care, I just wanted peace. I hurt so badly and knew my lustful self-righteous and self-willed way of doing things was the cause of my pain. Hope and I stayed in contact with one another and she would tell me how Anthony was drinking and doing drugs again and had a woman living with them. She was very disappointed with her daddy and did not like the destructive path he had chosen.

I was at home getting ready for bed when I got a call from Hope. She was crying so hard I couldn't understand what she was saying. I was able to calm her down and asked what was wrong. Hope told me that she was riding in the truck with her dad telling him that he needed to stop drinking and doing drugs and that he was wrong for doing it. She told me that Anthony did not like the things she was saying so he hit her in the face. She told me that she jumped out the truck and run to a nearby store where she called me.

There was a police officer there and saw Hope on the phone crying. He made sure she was safe and asked to talk to me. Hope gave the officer the phone and I told him who I was and that I would come pick her up. I called my sweet friend Esther and she drove me to get Hope. I was glad to see Hope and know that she was alright. I felt so sorry for her to have to witness her daddy's rage of anger. Hope didn't have any of her clothes so we decided that we would go to her house and get them.

The next day Hope and I drove to her house to get her clothes. She had told me there was a woman living there, but I didn't think much of it at the time. When we arrived, my spirit conscience told me to stay in the car and I did. Hope got out and knocked on the front door. No one answered so she went around to the back. She still got no answer. Well, I decided to get out and help her figure out a way to get into the house. We could not get in, so we decided to kick in the door. We didn't have to because the door opened and there stood a little petite woman. It was Anthony's girlfriend.

Hope and I walked into the house and went to her bedroom. There was a mattress on the floor where I assumed Hope slept and clothes were everywhere. I felt the anger in me rising as I walked into Anthony's room. His room was spotless, and bed covered with a black satin bedding set. Nothing was out of place. The woman didn't see me in the bedroom when she walked in and grabbed her undergarments out one of the drawers.

When I saw the bra, fury was my name. I grabbed a stick and began breaking anything I could. I pulled the bedding off onto the floor, his colognes, and his clothes. I left his room a mess and went into the living room. I broke ceiling fans windows and wanted to hit the woman. My spirit conscience said "Stop" and I did. I was furious. I talked to the little woman so crazy as she sat there shaking like a little mouse. Hope said, "I'm ready." We got into the car and left. That spirit conscience was saying "Didn't I tell you to stay in the car." I felt bad because I acted so horrible in front of Hope. Selfishly, I felt justified because he was my cheating husband.

Hope and I made it back to my house and I sat her down and told her that what we done was wrong. I also explained to her that I would need to send her back to her mom because her dad was not in his right mind to keep her. I wanted to keep Hope, but I couldn't because that would give Anthony a reason to come by whenever he wanted. I was not going to give him that control over me. Sending Hope back to her mother was sad for the both of us.

CHAPTER 23

Grace and Mercy

I WAS SORTING my mail when I noticed a piece from the Calvert County District Attorney office that was addressed to me. I opened the letter and to my surprise, Anthony had filed charges against me for the damages to his house. I had never been in trouble with the law, but I was now. The pending charges against me was for vandalism and malicious behavior. I could be facing one year in prison and up to ten thousand dollars in fines and costs.

Fear took hold of my mind. My heart was beating like a drum and I went into panic mode. I started begging God to please forgive me for what I had done. I begged him to please show grace, mercy, and favor over my situation. I imagined the consequences of my actions would be me going to prison. I could see my-self there witnessing to the inmates. "God have mercy on me" would be my daily quote. I was so ashamed of myself and remorseful for my actions. My self-righteous and self-willed way of doing things had led me into a situation out of my control.

I was sat down at church once again and didn't know what to do. I felt so silly. I read the court document again and decided to call the district attorney office. I needed to know what I could do to redeem myself. I called the office and was unable to reach anyone. I was very anxious and couldn't see no way out of this. I was guilty of the pending charges, so I steadied my mind by thinking about how doing God's work in prison would make the days more tolerable.

Documents came through the mail and informed me of my court date. I was so scared. How could I do something so stupid? I knew I had anger issues, but I never thought my anger would get me into any trouble. "God, where are you?" I asked. I was waiting on God to answer, but God was waiting on me to change. My sister Tonya went with me to court. When we made it there, I looked around for Anthony and the little woman to be there, but they weren't.

The judge entered the room, sat down and began to call out the case names. My knees knocked together underneath the long skirt I was wearing. My case number and name were called, and I slowly walked up front to face the judge. I could feel my knees nearly buckling and I had to hold on to the railing. The judge asked if the plaintiff, Anthony, was present? In my mind I thought it was over because Anthony wasn't there.

The judge continued and asked me if I understood the pending charges against me. I had a lump in my throat and couldn't say a word. I swallowed and said, "Yes sir." My hands were sweating, and my eyes filled with tears. The judge whispered something to an officer standing next to him and then the judge told me I needed to go to the jail and do a walk through. I didn't know where my strength or courage came from, but I raised my hand and asked the judge "Sir, am I going to prison?" The judge explained to me that I was not going to prison, but I needed to go next door to the police station.

I was relieved to know that I wasn't going to prison, but was I going to jail? What was a walk through? My sister and I went next door to the police station. When we arrived, I walked up to the front window and told the officer what the judge ordered me to do. I was told to sit down, and someone would be with me shortly. After sitting there for a while, a police officer called my name and I followed her to a room where she told me to sit down on this bench. There was a gentleman sitting there and I began to cry. He looked at me and said, "Your first time?" I cried harder.

An officer came to me and lead me to a room where I was photographed and fingerprinted. I had never felt so idiotic in my life. I couldn't leave, walk out, or say no. I was completely submissive and humbled by the courts. I did whatever the officer told me to do and was released to leave. When I walked out that room and was free, I went to my sister, grabbed her, and cried in her arms like a baby. She didn't know what to say so she just hugged me and told me it was going to be alright.

The ride home was slow and daunting. I made it through the preliminary court hearing, but the sentencing court date was still pending. The unknown was ahead of me. Days past and I was as meek as a little lamb. Embarrassment and shame walked ahead of me each time I went to church. I knew what I had done was wrong, but I needed encouragement, not judgement. My mind began to question some of the teachings I had learned, and I began to seek God with questions that I knew only he could answer. Something new was going on inside me and it felt right and good. My actions had awakened my heart to the fact that I was no better than anyone else. The

Love of God was saturating me with Grace and Mercy. I was no longer walking in fear. I was walking by Faith.

I called the district attorney office again and this time I was able to speak to him. I told him my case number and name and asked what I could do to get the pending charges against me dropped. I was told that Anthony would need to come into the office with one hundred fifty dollars and sign an affidavit and the case would be dropped. Hearing this news was hopeful, but how to get in touch with Anthony would be a challenge. He was not working, and I had no idea how to contact him. I trusted God.

I was working one day and out of the blue, Anthony called me. I started crying and he asked me what was wrong. I told him all that had happened to me at the police station. He apologized and asked if there was anything he could do to help. I told him what the district attorney told me. Anthony told me he would go sign the document, but I would need to pay the money. I paid the fee, he signed the document and all charges against me were dropped.

My self-righteous self-willed way of doing things could have cost me my job, and my freedom. God's Grace and Mercy brought me through.

CHAPTER 24

No Weapon Shall Prosper

I WAS THANKFUL and felt indebted to Anthony for dropping the charges against me. He was at the lowest point in his life that I had ever seen him. I wanted to do whatever I could to help him get back on the right path. Anthony would come by the house dirty, hungry, and tired. He would sleep for days and once rested, he would leave. It hurt me to see him like this and I partly blamed myself. if I hadn't put him out, maybe he would not be in this troubled shape.

I knew Anthony was drinking liquor again, but I had not witnessed it. One evening he came over and had a bottle with him. In the past, I would not let anyone drink liquor in my house. This time, I allowed Anthony to bring it in. He was pleasant, but the more he drank, his demeanor changed. I tried to play it cool, but his change bothered me. Anthony asked me if I would drive him to his house. I wanted to say no, but I felt he needed me, so I drove him.

Anthony was still drinking, and I thought he would eventually pass out. He was very tipsy and started bragging about how many young girls wanted him. To hear him talk like that made me feel sorry for him but it hurt me. I did not want him to know I was hurting so I just ignored him and told him I was ready to go home. Anthony had his phone in one hand, grabbed my arm and said, "Look at this." I had a feeling what it was and didn't want to look. He was very persistent and would not let me go, so I looked. Anthony had recorded himself having intercourse with another woman. I turned my face and felt like vomiting.

Anthony thought it was funny and tried to make me feel like I was wrong for not watching it. I felt so disrespected and degraded. He laughed again and said, "I'm going to the crack house." Anthony got in his truck and left me there alone. I needed to leave so I called my dear friend Esther. Esther picked me up and drove me home.

The next morning, I felt disgusted with myself. I should not have looked at the video when Anthony told me to. I went to work and was standing in front of the bathroom sink looking down. I began to cry when that spirit conscience said, "Hold your head up." I looked up, and in the mirror was a beautiful woman looking at me. That woman was me. Trying to love and support Anthony hurt, and the pain made me realize that my way, was not Gods way. I let Anthony go, refreshed, refocused, and concentrated on my relationship with God.

I was at home getting ready for choir rehearsal when there was a knock on the door. It was Anthony. I wanted to pretend as if I wasn't there, but he could see me through the window. Hesitantly, I allowed him to come in. Anthony sat down on the couch and we talked for a minute. Unforeseen, Anthony pulled out a pistol. I felt fear creeping in as he started mumbling to himself. I kindly told him I had choir rehearsal and asked him to leave. Without resist, He got up and walked out the door. I locked the door behind him.

SIMPLY TRUTH

I thought he was leaving but he didn't. Anthony beat on the door boldly, demanding that I open it. I told him to leave or I would call the police. He began to kick the door and it flew open. Before I could run, Anthony had grabbed me and threw me over a chair. He straddled me and held me down. I tried to scramble away from his grip, but I couldn't. He began to talk very crazy to me. I was in a panic and began to pray and quote scriptures out loud. Suddenly, Anthony released me, grabbed and broke my glasses, and walked out the door.

I was always afraid of guns. Now, it wasn't the gun I was afraid of, it was the man behind the gun. I walked around for days feeling like I was in danger, but I was not going to let anyone cause me to live in fear. I declared to myself that God was my shield and protector and I would not fear what man could do to me. I divorced Anthony and didn't see him again.

CHAPTER 25

Be not Deceived

WHEN I DIVORCED Anthony, the emotional pain was so intense that I felt it physically. Accepting the truth about myself was like being pierced with a knife. It hurt going in and it hurt coming out. The truth being, that broken young girl had grown into a broken adult woman. I wanted to believe that I was free from the emotional prison of my past, but I wasn't. My self-willed and self-righteous ways had held me captive. Each marriage I entered were like bandages that covered my wounds but did not heal them.

I felt so alone and full of pain. One morning before leaving for work, I got down on my knees and began to pray. I cried out to God and asked for strength. I asked God to forgive me of my sins, and to take the pain away. There was this warm feeling that came over me and I knew that only time would ease my pain. When I got up from my knees, I felt refreshed but still something was missing.

Being Blessed with my job was nothing short of a miracle. A miracle because it was the only place of employment within the small community where I resided. I was comfortable and pleased with my job and had no intentions of leaving. Living in a town with a population of about two hundred fifty people felt safe and reassuring for me. I was often asked the question, "When are you going to move out the country?" My answer would always be the same "Never!"

I began to have a desire to move away and had a tranquil dream that I did so. In the dream, I was living in California working at a post office. Realistically, the thought of moving anywhere tormented me. I was emotionally and spiritually handicapped by fear and did not realize it. For the next year, thoughts of moving would preoccupy my mind.

I was dispersing the mail at work when one of my customers named Cliff walled in. I spoke to him and he spoke back. We began a cordial conversation about the weather. He had this sad look on his face, and I asked, "Are you ok?" He told me that his wife had passed away. I felt compassion for his pain and gave him a hug. Each time he came in, the post office, we would greet one another and engage in pleasant conversation.

One morning Cliff came in to retrieve his mail. While there, he asked me if I would give him a call after work. I had this feeling that talking about the weather was not what he had in mind. After work, I called Cliff to see what the importance of my calling him was. Cliff asked me if I would have dinner with him that evening. My spirit conscience urged me to say yes but I declined. I had a business meeting to attend and used that as an excuse not to accept the invite. I did not want to go out to dinner with Cliff. The meeting was cancelled. Cliff was twice my age and going out to dinner with him was something I did not care to do. insistently, my spirit conscience was non-stop, so I called Cliff and told him I was free for dinner.

I want to dinner with Cliff and had a wonderful time. I learned that Cliff was a retired Pastor. With both of us being Christians, our dinner date conversation was even more gratifying. We began to spend time together and formed a friendship. I found myself caring very deeply for Cliff and believed he felt the same about me. Cliffs main place of residence was in California. He would spend his summer months at his vacation home in the country where I lived in my own home.

There were times when I would question my feelings about Cliff and did not understand how I fell in love with him because of our age difference. My spirit conscience would remind me that genuine Love had no color, gender, or boundaries. I knew in my heart this was all a part of Gods plan and purpose for me. After eighteen months of getting to know one another, Cliff asked me to marry him and I said yes. My mind went back to the peaceful dream I had of living in California. I exercised my Faith in God and overcame my fear. I was excited about the wedding and ready for the west coast move with Cliff.

I knew there would be no physical intimacy, but I loved Cliff, not what he could or could not do for me. I was looking forward to the spiritual companionship and friendship of our union.

CHAPTER 26

My Sixth Marriage

CLIFF AND I were in a long-distance relationship and planning our wedding. My over the phone evening conversations were a good way to end a long day of work. One evening as we talked, I felt something was bothering Cliff, so I asked him if he was ok. With him being much older than I, he wondered if my love for him was real or was there a hidden agenda behind it. Cliff asked me if I would sign a prenuptial agreement. I was self-supportive and content and didn't need anything from him. I told Cliff to send the papers and I would sign them. Cliff and I had a beautiful wedding ceremony.

I had all my clothes packed and ready to begin my new life. We were driving to California on the Interstate with traffic in front, back, and side. it began to rain hard and I asked Cliff to slow his speed. As he changed lanes the car hydroplaned. I was calling the name "Jesus! Jesus! Jesus! It amazed me how the car hit a guard rail head on, and instantly pinned sideways against the rail. The car never stopped moving forward and swiped the rail as it glided along.

Finally, the car was loosed, and we were able to pull over to the side of the interstate. I was shaken to my core and literally had just seen the end of my life flash before my eyes. My mind was on my children and grandchildren and how my death would have traumatized them. I was so scared, I considered hitch-hiking back home to the country. What had I gotten myself into? My spirit conscience said, "All things are working for your good, just trust me." Cliff and I got a room for the night. After twenty-two hours of driving, we made it home to California.

I was Thankful to be home. We were there for two days when Cliff found a repair shop to take the damaged vehicle. He told me that I would need to drive the spare car and follow him there. I was still shaken by the car incident and now my husband is counting on me to drive in five lanes of traffic! That night, I was restless and didn't get much sleep because I knew what was expected of me. The next morning, as the time came for me to follow my husband, I prayed and said, "Lord take the wheel." God gave me the strength and the courage to follow Cliff. I was more than elated when we made it to our destination and overwhelmed with joy when we made it back home.

I didn't realize just how fear controlled my life until I moved to California. The first year of Cliff and my marriage my focus was on him. I would follow Cliff as we traveled to a different church each Sunday. Very seldom did we attend the same place of worship consecutively. Cliff was getting all the love and attention he wanted, but I was starving for spiritual edification, and fellowship with other believers. I needed a stable place of worship where I could be an active member and work the gifts of ministry that God had given me.

Summer was coming and Cliff planned our vacation. We would drive to the country and on to other states to visit family and friends. We could have flown, but Cliff did not want that. The thought of riding twenty-two hours did not bring peace to my mind, but seeing my family was a good distraction from my fear. We headed out for the country and made it safely there without any incidents. After being in the country for a few weeks, we made our way to three other states. Meeting his family was beautiful, but the drive and ride was tedious.

I was emotionally fatigued when Cliff and I made it back to the country. Cliff told me that he was planning to go back to Missouri before leaving for California. I told him I did not feel the need to go and nothing else was said about it. We had been home for about a month when Cliff started planning his return trip to Missouri and wanted to know if I was going to make the drive with him. I said 'No, I am going to sit this one out." Cliff got very upset with me and told me I needed to leave his house and go back to my own. This was my first time seeing a side of Cliff that was not nice.

My saying "No" was a word I had not used with him. I packed my belongings and moved back into my house. I needed to have a heart to heart talk with God about this one. "God, what did I do wrong this time?" My reply was "You idolized a man." I had put Cliff on a pedestal and hinged on his every word. My heart had been Cliff centered and not God centered. Cliff's actions had thrown me for a loop, but I couldn't blame him for being the way he was. I needed to focus on my own faults.

CHAPTER 27

Gracefully Broken Still

I ASKED GOD to forgive me for the error of my way. I told God that I was willing and ready to do whatever he wanted me to do. My spirit conscience told me to go back to my husband. I couldn't see that happening because Cliff had put me out his house. The spirit conscience said to me "Trust Me." A few days past and Cliff called and apologized for his actions and how wrong he was. He told me he did not want to be without me. Cliff made it back to the country and picked me up from my house. He comforted my mind by saying he would never treat me that way again. I heard what Cliff said, but my mind was aimed at listening to and obeying God. We stayed in the country for a few more weeks and then drove back to California.

I was glad to be off the interstate, and safely back in California. I remembered what I had told God and waited for him to send me where he wanted me to be. I had no friends and had never been anywhere without Cliff. God would allow my path to cross with diverse people and I would get an invite to various church activities. I was joyful about getting out fellowshipping with other believers, but Cliff was not thrilled about my going. I had made the mistake of putting him before God once and I was not going to to that again.

I met a sweet beautiful lady named Tracy and formed a beautiful friendship with her. Tracy invited me to visit her church. She was on the praise and worship team there. I visited the church and Unexpectedly, it was the first church Cliff had taken me to when I moved to California. I felt a connection on my first visit there. This was my second time and I knew this is where God wanted me to be. The Word of God taught and the community outreach there were awesome.

I did not know it, but the pastor of the church had been praying for a praise, worship, and choir leader. Singing being my passion, I knew I was on track with Gods will and purpose. The members of Pleasant Grace were very loving and kind. I felt I had known them all my life. I started going to Pleasant Grace on a regular basis when I decided to become a member. Out of respect to my husband, I talked to him about it. Cliff said that I could do what I wanted but he did not recommend it. I took that as his blessing and joined Pleasant Grace.

I worked in the music department and where ever needed very delighted and care free. Our music team was invited to minister through praise and worship at another church. Cliff came and was sitting in the pulpit. As I got up to sing, I acknowledged my pastor, my husband, and all the other dignitaries in the pulpit. The praise, worship, and Word of God was dynamic, and I was overflowing with joy in doing what I loved to do. My husband being there made me feel even more blessed.

On our ride home from the service, I was so excited and talked about how I enjoyed the service. Cliff was very quiet. When we got home, Cliff began to tell me how wrong I was for acknowledging my pastor at the service. I had never seen him so angry. He reminded me that he was my husband and that no other man should be acknowledged but him. Cliff told me that he did not marry me and bring me to California to help anyone but him. He told me that since I joined Pleasant Grace, they needed to take care of me because I was no longer a wife of his. Cliff filed for a divorce.

I was astonished. Where was this coming from and what happened to the God loving gentlemen I married? The man standing in front of me that could quote scriptures from the bible front to back was cold hearted, mean, and ugly. In spite of what I was seeing and hearing, I believed this marriage was a part of Gods plan for my good.

CHAPTER 28

A Friend Indeed

I TALKED TO some of my friends at church about my situation but the more I talked, the worse I felt. My spirit conscience said, "Stop talking about it, trust me, and Pray."

I believed in prayer and would pray but I would become a prayer warrior through this. I began to get on my knees and pray and prayer became my meat day and night. My friendship with God grew into an intimate and personal relationship. The good parts in all six of my previous marriages, never made me feel as good as my intimacy with God. I prayed for myself more than I did Cliff. I needed the strength to go through the pain with joy and peace. I needed God to shine in me and be glorified through me.

I was sitting on the bed studying my bible when Cliff walked in to the room. He kept a pistol in the nightstand next to the bed. He walked over to the night stand and pulled the pistol and bullets out as if he was going to load the gun. I felt fear, but, that quiet spirit conscience said, "Fear not, quote Psalms 23 out loud" I began to quote Psalms 23 as I walked toward Cliff.

"The Lord is my shepherd; I shall not want. He makes me to lie down in green pastures; he leads me beside the still waters. He restores my soul; he leads me in the paths of righteous for his name's sake. Yea, though I walk through the valley of the shadow of death, I will fear no evil; for You are with me; Your rod and Your staff they comfort me. You prepare a table before me in the presence of my enemies; You anoints my head with oil; my cup runs over. Surely goodness and mercy shall follow me All the days of my life; and I will dwell in the house of the LORD Forever.

I felt no fear. As I sat back down on the bed, Cliff put the gun back in the drawer and walked out the room. Cliff was so bitter and angry towards me and no matter how much I loved and cared for him, he rejected any kindness I showed him. I never ceased to pray. The more I prayed, the more meek, gentle, and patient I became. Cliff, however, seemed to become more wicked and evil.

Cliff left for the weekend and came home after a few days. He walked over to the bed where I was and touched me. His hands were cold as ice and he looked as if something had scared him. He said, "I do not want a divorce." That was good news for me because I didn't want one either. The next morning, we went to his paralegal and he told her he wanted to discard the divorce papers.

I didn't know what made Cliff change his mind and I didn't ask. I kept praying and seeking God each day. Another summer was approaching, and Cliff wanted to leave for vacation to the country a month earlier than we usually left. I had a musical concert coming up and asked if we could leave afterwards. Cliff told me no so I asked him if I could stay and come later. Cliff told me that he was not going to leave me in his house and if I didn't come with him, he was going to file for divorce. I didn't think Cliff was serious.

SIMPLY TRUTH

A few weeks later, my spirit conscience led me to call the paralegal. I called and asked if Cliff had filed for divorce and she had. I wasn't surprised, but I was disappointed. Cliff behavior towards me was so mean that I moved into the spare bedroom. He disconnected my cell phone, dropped my medical insurance, and cut me off from any resources. Emotionally, I hurt. I was alone in this big city with no family, finances, and completely out of my comfort zone. Spiritually, I felt stronger than I had ever felt in all the years of my adulthood. God was with me all the time.

CHAPTER 29

Way Maker

I HAD NO income, no phone, no medical insurance, and no transportation. The person I had completely depended upon had turned his back on me. Cliff wanted me to leave his house. I wanted to, but my spirit conscience would tell me to wait. I needed to learn the bus and train system but that would be fearful and difficult due to my low vision. I couldn't read the bus signs nor the stop lights to know which but to get on or when to cross the street. I had to depend on God, and I did.

I had been to several optometrist seeking help for my eyes. The last one I went to, referred me to a retinal specialist. I was very optimistic. When I arrived for my appointment, I was taken into a room to watch a film about methods used for retina repair. For the first time in my life, I would be able to see everything. Upon completion of the film and many tests, the doctor came into the room where I was waiting. He sat down, looked at me, and said "Do you want the good new first or the bad news?"

I wasn't prepared to hear any bad news. The doctor told me that I had nerve damage to my retina and there was nothing that could be done to repair it. He told me the good news was that I wasn't going blind. My hopes of ever being able to see normally was gone. I began to cry uncontrollably.

The doctor was so kind and apologetic as if it were his fault. I regained my composer as the doctor told me he would do whatever necessary to help me get disability assistance. I had been this way all my life and never felt disabled. I thanked the kind doctor and cried all the way home.

On top of everything else I was going through, I felt my mind going to a place of self-pity. I didn't know how much more I could handle. I got down on my knees and begin to pray. First, I thanked God for my eyes and then for his strength. I didn't know how God was going to work through my circumstances, but I trusted Him. Cliff had given me jewelry and reluctantly, I began to sell the jewelry and buy the things I needed.

Tracy was familiar with the area and would drive me to sell my jewelry. One day she asked me if I had applied for state assistance. I didn't think I would be eligible for assistance having a husband and no child. I called and scheduled an appointment anyway. I went to my appointment and was assigned a case worker. I told my case worker about my pending divorce and my situation. To my surprise, I was eligible for cash, medical, and food stamps. I received one hundred ninety dollars in cash and two hundred two dollars in food stamps.

I had received my state allotment for the month and had one hundred dollars left. My spirit conscience told me to open a bank account. I wondered why I needed a bank account, but I obeyed. I went to the closest bank and opened a checking account. A few days later, my spirit conscience told me to go and apply for disability. I was skeptical about this move because I knew people who had applied and got denied.

I trusted God and obeyed. Tracy drove me to the social security office and helped me fill out the paperwork. I went to the back and sat down with one of the workers to go over my application. The worker asked me "Do you have a bank account?" I had just opened my account two days before. I knew in my heart that every step of my moving to California was ordained and approved by God.

CHAPTER 30

The Fiery Furnace

EACH DAY WOULD get harder to live in the house with Cliff. He was so bitter and angry. Outwardly he was like a sheep but inwardly, he was like a wolf. Cliff had planned to leave for vacation to the country early in March. He didn't realize that once he filed for the divorce, the hearing would be scheduled for July. I knew there was a possibility that I would have to move back to my country home and that was not a happy thought. I loved being in California.

Days passed and I began to walk in my hurt feelings. I was not praying as often and focused on my problems more than on God. Cliff was becoming more and more unbearable. I had step family across town and was offered a place to stay when the divorce was granted. They were leaving for vacation a few days before my divorce hearing. A suggestion was made that I could move in and be there to watch the house and the dogs while they were gone.

My spirit conscience said, "Wait and stand still." I was so engulfed in my feelings, that I failed to be obedient to the spirit. I moved in with my step family. They flew out for vacation on July second and I went to my divorce hearing on July seventh. Surprisingly, due to discrepancies in the paperwork that Cliff filed, the judge dismissed the case and told Cliff he would need to get an attorney. I was relieved but felt foolish because I had disobeyed my spirit conscience and got ahead of God. I was still married to Cliff. My step family made it home from vacation and I left for the country to visit my family.

I enjoyed spending time with my loved ones, but I was ready to leave for California. I called my step family to let them know when I would be back. It was made clear that I would have to return to the place of pain that I was running from. My spirit conscience told me to go back to Cliff house. I wanted to go back to California, but not to Cliff house. That house was not a place of refuge for me but turmoil and emotional torture. I humbled myself, obeyed my spirit conscience, and returned.

It was around seven thirty on a Sunday morning when I arrived at the house. I tried to unlock the door to enter, but my key did not work. I could hear someone inside the house. I called out Cliff's name and he answered, "You are not coming in here." I replied, "I am still your wife and you need to let me in." Cliff refused to open the door. My spirit conscience said, "Didn't I tell you to wait and stand still." I couldn't get mad because I was wrong for leaving. I sat outside the house for three hours in the heat.

My children had given me money before I left for California, so I decided to call a locksmith. The locksmith arrived and attempted to remove the lock from the door. Cliff yelled out, "if you don't leave my door alone, I am going to shoot you." The poor locksmith was so frightened he took off without saying a word. I knew Cliff would be leaving for church soon, so I just sat and waited. After waiting another hour, a car pulled up and Cliff walked out he house. Cliff looked at me as he passed me by, got into the car, and left. I was frustrated and hot. My spirit conscience reminded me, again, "Didn't I tell you to wait, and stand still?" I couldn't think or say anything but "God, I am sorry, please forgive me."

I walked around to the back door to see if Cliff had forgotten to lock it. The door was locked, but I remembered how I would open the bathroom window for fresh air. The window was down, but I needed to check to see if it was locked. It was a small window that was high off the ground. I found a chair to stand in, but I still wasn't tall enough to reach the window. I looked around and found a wooden box. I put the box inside the chair and was able to check the window. It was unlocked.

I opened the window and was ready to climb through with phone in my back pocket. I jumped and pulled my upper body through the small window and heard the box fall out the chair. I tried to pull the rest of my body through, but my phone lodged against the window and prevented me from moving. I couldn't go back out because there was no foundation underneath my feet. I was stuck halfway through the window. I felt like I was going to die from suffocation. I started yelling "Help, somebody help me." The more I yelled, the shorter by breaths.

One of my neighbors heard me yelling and came to my rescue. He removed my phone, lifted my lower body, and I was able to pull myself through the window. I made it through and needed to get my luggage from outside the house. I couldn't get out. Cliff had not only changed the outside locks, but he had installed inside locks that required a key to open.

CHAPTER 31

A Way Out

HOW WAS I to get out the house? The only way was to break out. I looked for something to use and found a hammer and crowbar and forced the door open. I walked outside, got my luggage, and went back to my room. The room I was told not to leave from the beginning. I did not know how Cliff was going to react when he returned home but I was prepared. I unpacked my things and called another locksmith. I was not going to be locked out again. The gentleman that came to change the lock was very tall, muscular, and kind.

While the locksmith was changing the lock, Cliff came in from church. He walked up and asked the man what he was doing. The gentleman turned and looked at Cliff and said, "I'm changing the lock." Cliff didn't say another word but walked past and went into the house. I went into my room to digest all that had happened. I tried to avoid Cliff the rest of the day, but he was angry, and verbally threatened me.

I was tired from the day's drama and went to bed early. I was lying in bed when I heard a knock on my bedroom door. I said "Come in." I could see a very large police officer standing in my doorway. I just knew I was going to jail for breaking and entering. The officer stepped in my room and asked me "Are you Mrs. Strong and do you live here?" I told him I did, and I had just come home from vacation. He said, "OK mam, sorry to bother you." The officer walked out and closed the door. Cliff thought by calling the police I would be removed from the home. My spirit conscience told me to file a restraint order against Cliff. I didn't feel I was in danger, but I obeyed. The next morning, I called Tracy and she drove me to the court house.

As I was walking in, Cliff was walking out. He had filed one against me to have me removed from his house. The restraint order had eighteen different headings and he had checked all eighteen of them. I checked the heading for restraint against verbal and emotional abuse. We went to court and both restraints were dismissed. The judge told Cliff once again that if he wanted me out the house he would need to file for divorce.

Cliff retained an attorney and filed. I had my strategy all planned out and called around and spoke to attorneys. There was one that stood out from the others. I made an appointment to see him, caught the bus, and went to his office. While speaking with the attorney, I learned that he was born and raised sixty miles from my home town and had moved to California. We were both from the same state. He was the right attorney for me. He told me what I could do to prepare myself and instructed me on how to do it.

I made it back home and thought on what the attorney told me. I had been through too much suffering and pain not to be compensated. My spirit conscience said "You will not ask for anything other than what you brought in." I did not want to hear that. My thoughts were not pretty. Anger, bitterness, and unforgiveness I fed on daily, but I smiled. I would periodically receive documents from Cliff's attorney regarding the divorce and that made me angrier.

Cliff was leaving for the labor-day weekend. One of my friends from church had made plans and I wanted to join in. I called the bank to check my account. When the teller told me my balance, I was confused. I told her that the bank must have put money in my account by mistake. She asked me if I was expecting a deposit to post. I told her that I had applied for social security benefits, but I had not received an approval or denial letter.

When the teller told me there was a deposit posted from the federal treasury, I was speechless. God had approved my social security benefits. Six months I was on state assistance while I waited. It's amazing how it all worked together. I was scheduled for a renewal interview and was able to tell my case worker I needed no further assistance from the state.

Later in the next week, I received a document from Cliff's attorney about the court date. It was scheduled for January 22, 2016. The thought of moving back to the country made me sick to my stomach. My spirit conscience was comforting, but my self-will fought against the spirit.

CHAPTER 32

Time Told the Story

I BEGAN LOOKING at apartments determined that I was not leaving California. Every door seemed to close in my face. I was not accepting a move back to the country. Going back would mean that I had failed in another marriage.

My friend Tracy did not want me to move back either so she would drive me around to look at apartments. We were driving around one day, when I got weak, my heart raced, and I broke out in a sweat. Felt like my body was shutting down. I told Tracy I was having a heart attack and told her to take me to the hospital. She could tell something was wrong because my speech wasn't clear. I described my symptoms and Tracy told me I was having an anxiety attack.

My daughter Faith called while this was happening. I answered the phone and told her I was having a heart attack. Tracy told her my symptoms and they both agreed that it was an anxiety attack. I was praying within asking God to please touch my body and telling him what I would do if he did. The closer we got to the hospital, the better I felt. Tracy and my daughter were right. I had an anxiety attack.

I got all the notions of staying in California out my head. I accepted going back home to the country, but I was not happy about it. I told Cliff I needed plastic tubs to start packing. The date for the divorce hearing came and I went. There was a litigator, Cliff and his attorney, and me. I don't know what Cliff told his attorney about me. The woman the attorney described me as was cruel, evil, and conniving. All I could do was sit there and cry. The litigator asked me what I wanted. I told her the only compensation I wanted was what I brought into the marriage.

We had reached an agreement and ready to go before the judge. The judge told me that I needed to leave the premises and asked me how much time I needed to pack. I told the judge two weeks would be plenty of time. I wore a smile, but I hurt so badly. I went home and began packing. The hardest part about leaving California was the friends I had made. My time in California when I needed Love, support, encouragement, and edification, was met by my sisters and brothers at Pleasant Grace Praise Center. God knew all along the plans he had for me.

Moving back to Oklahoma was in Gods perfect time. I was not sent back to my country home. God sent me to help my daughter Faith. I moved in with my daughter and was there for her when she needed me the most. I was tired, broken, and felt abused. I needed a place of worship. A place of refuge. I had visited Saving Lives church before I moved to California and told myself I would not go back there again. My self-righteous way of thinking had been judgmental and hypocritical. God sent me back to Saving Life church.

Each time I went to church, I cried and cried. My tears were like water washing me from the inside out. The leadership, teaching, and preaching at Saving Life church was phenomenal. The deepest issues of my heart that had never been addressed were now being healed by the Word of God.

My life was changing bits and pieces at a time. The pieces that I held on to were anger and unforgiveness.

I had done a favor for someone and I felt they had wronged me. In my angered state of mind. I posted a message on social media about the person. I tried to dress it up, but the underlining was ugly. I went to church that Sunday morning and when I walked through the door, I felt like I was standing there in my birthday suit. My spirit conscience told me "The light of your anger and unforgiveness is shining brighter than the light of me in your life." All the ugliness inside me was being unconverd. In all my years of faithful church attendance and hearing the Word of God, I had failed to live the Word of God. I dressed and looked Godly, as society portrays Godly, but I needed a God heart transplant.

I lived my life exercising the works of the flesh. Anger, fear, envy, unforgiveness, hypocrisy, and idolatry. I had been a stumbling block in front of my family, friends, and strangers. For the first time in my life, my heart was broken and contrite. I felt sorry for all the times I failed Jesus Christ my Savior. I was tired of doing things my way. I was tired of repeating the same cycles. Finally, I had learned that my life was not my own to live my way. I wanted to be a new creation in Christ. I repented of my sins and asked Jesus to come into my heart. In all my years of attending church, this was my first real experience of feeling worthy to be called a born-again believer. I am a new creation in Christ.

CONCLUSION

1 JOHN 2:16 "For all that is in the world, the lust of the flesh, the lust of the eyes, and the pride of life is not of the Father but is of the world. {17} and the world is passing away, and the lust of it; but he who does the will of God abides forever.

From the date of my conception, God had a plan and a purpose for my life. I was born into a family void of God's Love, knowledge, wisdom, and understanding. A family that stemmed from a broken root. Bitter does not yield sweet, evil does not yield good. In either case, the seeds planted, will bring forth one or the other. I had no identity or foundation to build on other than what I seen and heard. The thing that society labels as "Generational Curses." I was a lost soul until I heard about Jesus Christ.

> John 3:16-17 "For God so loved the world that he gave His only begotten Son; that whoever Believes in Him should not perish but have everlasting life. {17} For God did not send His Son into the world to condemn the world, but that the world through Him might be saved.
>
> Romans 10:9 "That if you confess with your mouth the Lord Jesus and believe in your heart that God has raised Him from the dead, you will be saved.

Confessing and believing in him, saved me from sin and I became a newborn believer. That was only the start. I needed guidance in learning what it meant to be a new creation in Christ. The Holy Bible was the instruction manual but immature leadership was detrimental to my spiritual growth. For thirty years of my life, I was spiritually stunted. It was time for my spiritual break through. There is a time for everything under the sun. God sent me to a place where He knew I would be changed. Being fed biblically with clarity made all the difference in my life.

> Romans 12:1-2 "I beseech ye therefore brethren by the mercies of God, that you present your bodies a living sacrifice, holy, acceptable to God, which is your reasonable service. {2} And do not be conformed to this world, but, be transformed by the renewing of your mind that you may prove what is that good and acceptable and perfect will of God.

I am a walking testimony of how God changed a me, myself, and I Christian, to a "For God I live for God I die." Believer.

> 2 Corinthians 5:17 "If anyone is in Christ, he is a new creation; old thing have passed away; behold, all things have become new.
> I Peter 4:1 "Therefore since Christ suffered for us in the flesh, arm yourselves also with the same mind, for he who has suffered in the flesh

has ceased from sin, {2} That he no longer lives the rest of his time in the flesh for the lusts of men, but for the will of God.

On my own I am nothing, but with God I can do all things. Each day that I live I will Trust in the Lord with all my heart and lean not on my own understanding. In all my ways I will acknowledge Him and He will direct my path. Now you know the story, behind my praise.

CPSIA information can be obtained
at www.ICGtesting.com
Printed in the USA
BVHW032212140419
545515BV00002B/12/P

———